The Merchant and the Thief

A FOLKTALE OF GODLY WISDOM

RAVI ZACHARIAS

ILLUSTRATED BY LAD ODELL

Chariot Victor Publishing
A Division of Cook Communications

Chariot Victor Publishing
a division of Cook Communications, Colorado Springs, Colorado 80918
Cook Communications, Paris, Ontario
Kingsway Communications, Eastbourne, England

THE MERCHANT AND THE THIEF
© 1999 by Ravi Zacharias for text and Lad Odell for illustrations

All rights reserved. Except for brief excerpts for review purposes,
no part of this book may be reproduced or used in any form
without written permission from the publisher.

Designed by Big Cat Marketing Communications
Edited by Kathy Davis
Creative Direction by Kelly S. Robinson

First hardcover printing, 1999
Printed in the United States of America
03 02 01 00 99   5 4 3 2 1

Library of Congress Cataloging-in-Publication Data

Zacharias, Ravi K.
     The merchant and the thief: a folktale of godly wisdom / by Ravi Zacharias;
illustrated by Lad Odell.
                    p.   cm.
     Summary: In this version of an Indian folktale, a thief travels with a wealthy jewel
merchant and tries and fails several times to uncover and steal his treasures,
but in return the merchant offers the thief God's forgiveness and a life in Jesus Christ.
     ISBN 0-7814-3296-0
     [1. Robbers and outlaws Fiction. 2. India Fiction. 3. Christian life Fiction.]
I. Odell, Lad, ill.   II. Title.
PZ7.Z167Mg 1999
[Fic] — dc21   99-20997
                                                                CIP

This book belongs to:

_____

"Do not store up for yourselves treasures on earth, where moth and rust destroy, and where thieves break in and steal. But store up for yourselves treasures in heaven, where moth and rust do not destroy, and where thieves do not break in and steal. For where your treasure is, there your heart will be also" Matthew 6:19-21 (NIV).

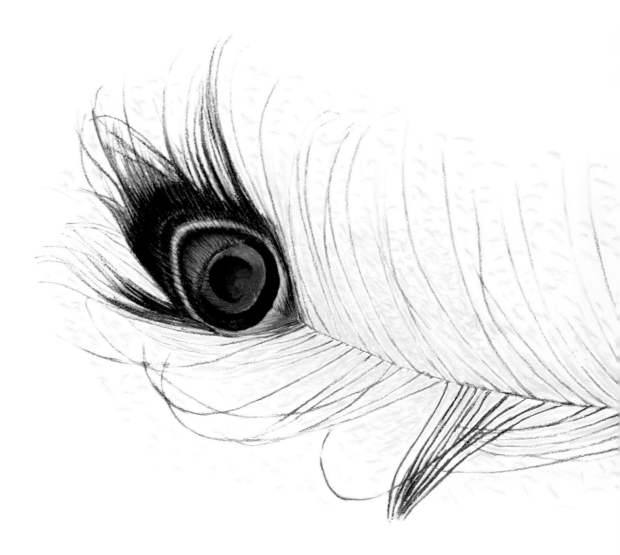

In a small, crowded town in India, a wealthy jewel merchant lived with his wife and three children. The town was very unusual, for most of the houses were painted pink. Therefore, everyone called it "the pink town." The rich man's name was Raj, and he lived in a big white house surrounded by a fence with a low iron gate.

The evening meal was a special time in this house. Raj's family would spread a mat on the floor and sit with their legs crossed beneath them. They ate hot, spicy meals using flat bread called *chapatis* to pick up their food, which is the custom in India. They would talk and laugh about things that happened to them during the day, and Raj often told favorite stories from his childhood.

Although Raj lived a happy life, he had also known great sadness, for his own parents had died in an accident a few years before. That is when Raj had inherited their jewelry business and had become quite wealthy.

A man named Mohan also lived in the pink town. He did not have much money, for he was a seller of fruits and vegetables. Every morning he woke up early and went to the market to buy the best produce he could find to sell to housewives and their servants at their gates. He put everything into a big basket, lifted the basket onto his head, and carried it from house to house.

*M*ohan also had a lovely family, but he wished he could do more for them. His children did not often have the tasty foods that Raj's children had, and sometimes they even left the table a little hungry. When he stood outside the big houses selling his vegetables, he wished he could have such a home. When he watched his children playing in the narrow street outside his little house, he wanted so much to give them a garden to play in. And often Mohan was too tired at the end of the day to laugh and play with his children.

Mohan began to think to himself, *I want to be rich like the people who live in those big houses.* The more he dreamed of all the things he wanted, he started to steal little things. Sometimes he took a little money from his neighbors. Sometimes he took extra vegetables from the market so he would have more to sell. And sometimes he did not give enough change to his customers. Before he realized it, he had become a thief waiting to steal something big.

$\mathcal{N}$ow Mohan had been peddling his goods in Raj's neighborhood for many years. He knew that every year Raj went on a long journey to visit his brothers and sisters in the town where he was born. Mohan reasoned that Raj would take his most precious jewels with him to keep them safe.

Mohan began to think about those jewels, and one day he had a brilliant idea: This year when Raj made his journey, Mohan would follow him and steal his fortune.

$\mathcal{O}$n the day of his trip Raj did indeed pack his most treasured jewels in his bag. These were things that Raj would never sell—his mother's diamond wedding ring, a diamond and sapphire necklace he was saving for his daughter's eighteenth birthday, and a gold bracelet he had chosen to surprise his wife. There were many other precious pieces, as well as gifts for his sisters and brothers.

So with his bag in one hand and a walking stick in the other, Raj said good-bye to his family and began to walk at a steady pace so he could reach the next village by the end of the day.

Meanwhile, Mohan dressed in his best clothes so Raj would not guess how poor he really was. He also kissed his family good-bye and set out to follow Raj. Before long Mohan was walking beside Raj and acting very friendly toward him.

At first Raj did not suspect that Mohan was planning to rob him, but he soon began to mistrust Mohan. He knew that the small roadside inns had few rooms and too many guests. Often two or more travelers had to share the same room, and he might be expected to share a room with Mohan. So Raj secretly made a plan to protect his treasure—and to teach Mohan an important lesson.

That evening they stopped at a little inn, and as Raj expected they were given a room to share.

The innkeeper gave each of the men a mat and a pillow. He also gave each a towel, a basin, and soap to clean up before bed.

As the men began to unpack their bags, Mohan watched carefully out of the corner of his eye to see if Raj would take his jewels out of his bag. When Raj did not, Mohan quickly thought of a clever plan. *I'll go out on the porch to wash my face. Then, when I return and Raj leaves the room, I'll find the jewels and run off into the night.*

But Raj had a plan of his own. While Mohan was outside, Raj hid his treasure in a place where he was sure the thief would never look.

When Mohan returned and Raj went out onto the porch, Mohan immediately raced to Raj's bag and searched frantically for the jewels. He dug his hands into the pockets of the bag and between the layers of clothing, but he could not find any treasure there. He began to get angry, for he was sure the jewels must be in the bag. Perhaps in his rush he had not looked carefully enough. *I'll find those jewels tomorrow*, he thought to himself as Raj returned.

The next evening when they stopped at another inn, they again shared a room. When Mohan went out to the porch to clean up, Raj hid the jewels once more.

This time Mohan was certain he knew where the treasure was hidden. When Raj left the room, Mohan tip-toed over to his belongings and searched hurriedly under Raj's pillow. Again he found nothing. Now he was really upset.

The same thing happened each night. Mohan searched in Raj's bag, under his mat, and even in his trouser pockets. In the middle of the night, while Raj was sound asleep and snoring heavily, Mohan quietly slipped out of his bed and searched in the wastebasket and under every piece of furniture in the room. Indeed, he had searched in everything the rich man owned, but he could not find the jewels! He began to wonder if he had been mistaken about Raj having any treasure at all.

On the last afternoon of their journey, Raj put his hands on Mohan's shoulders and looked into his eyes. "Mohan," he said, "I want to let you in on a little secret. I know why you pretended to be my friend. You wanted my jewels. Although you thought you looked everywhere for them, there is one place you did not look. The treasure was nearer to you than you thought, for it was under your own pillow all the time."

*M*ohan was shocked to think that every night he had laid his head on the treasure, yet he had never thought to look so close to himself.

"When we have our eyes on other people's riches," Raj said, "we cannot see how close we are to the greatest treasure there is. Anyone can have that treasure—even you, Mohan."

For the first time, Mohan stopped to think about what he had become. He had once been a poor but honest man. He thought of all his blessings—his wife and children, his job, his friends. Those were riches money could not buy. Feeling ashamed, Mohan knelt down at Raj's feet and begged his forgiveness. "But what is the *greatest* treasure?" he asked earnestly.

Raj helped Mohan to his feet. "The greatest treasure is God's love for you, my friend. He is willing to forgive you and make you a rich man on the inside."

Mohan looked puzzled. "What do you mean by 'rich on the inside'?"

Raj took out a small Bible and showed Mohan that God had given His best to him—the gift of His Son Jesus Christ. He explained that when you give your life to Christ, God makes you His own child. God loves His children and cares for their every need.

Mohan was overcome with joy. "How good it is to know that God cares for me and my family. I, too, want that treasure, God's love, in my heart."

As they parted later that evening, the men embraced and Mohan thanked Raj for sharing the greatest treasure with him. From now on, Mohan would look to God for his needs.

They went in separate directions—Raj toward his birthplace and Mohan back to his home. Mohan was happier than he had ever been before because he had found a far greater treasure than gold or jewels.